ORIGINALLY PUBLISHED BY
HARVARD UNIVERSITY PRESS

The Bill of Rights

by Learned Hand

THE OLIVER WENDELL HOLMES LECTURES, 1958

INTRODUCTION BY
Charles E. Wyzanski, Jr.

Atheneum   *New York*
1977

ACKNOWLEDGMENT

The passage from Aristotle's Ethica Nichomachea on pages 21-22 is from the translation by W. D. Ross, and the passage from the Rhetorica on pages 22-23 is from the translation by W. Rhys Roberts, in *The Works of Aristotle,* vols. IX and XI, translated into English under the editorship of W. D. Ross (Oxford: At the Clarendon Press, 1925, 1924), quoted by permission of the publisher.

Published by Antheneum
Reprinted by arrangement with Harvard University Press
Copyright © 1958 by the President and Fellows of
Harvard College
Introduction copyright © 1963 by Charles E. Wyzanski, Jr.
All rights reserved
ISBN 0-689-70085-7
Manufactured in the United States of America by
Halliday Lithograph Corporation, West Hanover, Massachusetts
Published in Canada by McClelland & Stewart Ltd.
First Atheneum Printing December 1963
Second Printing August 1965
Third Printing September 1968
Fourth Printing January 1972
Fifth Printing September 1974
Sixth Printing September 1977

INTRODUCTION

CHARLES E. WYZANSKI, JR.

No commentator on the United States Constitution has a better title to be heard than Judge Learned Hand. When he delivered these Holmes lectures in his eighty-seventh year, he was universally acknowledged as the greatest living judge in the English-speaking world, and was greeted by an overflow audience unmatched in law-school history.

Part of his reputation sprang from the distinction with which he served in the Federal courts during an unprecedented tenure, from 1909 to 1961. No lower court judge was so often cited by name in opinions of the Supreme Court of the United States or in academic publications. None in so few strokes could etch the growth of a legal principle, or reveal, without massive, pretentious quotation, its cultural and philosophical import. Justice Holmes had written that he would have welcomed him as a colleague; and the press spoke of him as the Tenth Justice of the Supreme Court.

Even more of Judge Hand's general public acclaim was attributable to the felicity with which he addressed ceremonial gatherings. His speech lent "a lustre and more great opinion, a larger dare to our great enterprise." His vision, unrestricted by boundaries of partisanship, provinciality, or narrow mores, had an inclusive wisdom. His Shakespearean understanding of the range of the human spirit was reflected in his magnificent countenance. Sometimes, as in the unforgettably gay portrait by Gardner Cox, Judge Hand revealed the robust joy that made men seek his companionship in their happiest hours. At other times, as in the photographs taken by Eleanor Platt and in her bust of him, Judge Hand reflected his profound awareness that "Suffering is permanent, obscure and dark, And shares the nature of infinity."

The character of Judge Hand was perfectly mirrored in his theories of jurisprudence. Subscribing to Montaigne's skepticism, *"Que scais-je?"*, he had never discovered any immutable principles of natural justice, and doubted if any existed. Nor if he found them would he as judge have been prepared to import them into the system of positive law which he was commissioned to apply. He saw the law, certainly in its enacted form, and often in its common law forms, as principally a reflection of compromises among competing interests. No doubt he would have agreed that law owed much to tradition, to reason, to ideals; yet in the end he would have accepted the Hobbesian declaration that "Power and Appetite are the two sides of Commodity." He would have acknowledged that "Clubs are trumps," if there were added a clause stipulating that inquiry could be directed as to the authority by which the clubs were wielded.

Judge Hand's view of the judge was austere, even Austinian. He regarded it as his chief obligation to be a disinterested interpreter of other men's wills. He was to remain detached, not merely from immediate partisanship, but also from any ultimate passion for reform. Such abstinence he regarded as the only condition upon which appointed judges could properly be tolerated in a democracy. For judges to offer themselves as Platonic guardians would wrongly lead the laity to expect of judges more than they could perform, and would impair such limited authority as they might properly enjoy.

INTRODUCTION

Holding these jurisprudential views, Hand readily accepted the constitutional law doctrines of his law school professor, James Bradley Thayer, who taught that it would discourage the citizenry from bearing its fair share of political responsibility if courts, except in the plainest cases, exercised a jurisdiction to invalidate a legislative choice. Indeed, in 1908, the year before he became a District Judge, Learned Hand wrote in the Harvard Law Review that the Supreme Court's use of the "due process" clause to invalidate legislation governing hours of work was a "usurpation" and that where a statute is not "obviously oppressive and absurd," but is "fairly within the field of rational discussion and interest" the Constitution gives no authority to the Supreme Court to set aside the legislative judgment.

Half a century later in these Holmes lectures, Judge Hand elaborates the same views. He asserts that the only reason that the Supreme Court has any veto is because if the Constitution were not to fail it became necessary to add to the text a power in the Court to act as arbiter among competing governmental authorities. But this necessity does not, and the first ten amendments and the Fourteenth Amendment do not, furnish any basis for any judicial declaration of unconstitutionality once the Court has determined that a matter lies within the boundary of a particular governmental authority, be it Congress, or President, or State. The Court is not authorized to reweigh what a competent authority has weighed.

The power which the Court has exercised under the "due process" clauses to annul "arbitrary," "unreasonable," or "discriminatory" laws, Judge Hand declares, does not lend itself "to any definition that will explain when the Court will assume the role of a third legislative chamber . . . I have never been able to understand on what basis it does or can rest except as a *coup de main.*" Judge Hand not only denies that courts have a legitimate power to annul unreasonable laws, he believes that for them to exercise such power promotes political appointments to the bench, encourages dissenting opinions revealing to the laity how much of the law is debatable, and, contrary to democratic principles, vests ultimate power in a small unrepresentatively selected group of persons.

Despite his erudition, beauty of expression, and poignant invocation of traditional ideals, Judge Hand's thesis has not yet been supported by a single eminent judge or professor. And, paradoxically, he himself was unwilling to have United States Senators cite these lectures as proof that the segregation cases represented judicial usurpation. Nonetheless, as McGeorge Bundy, then Dean of Harvard's Faculty of Arts and Science, affirmed in his review in the Yale Law Journal, these lectures are destined "to become a permanent part of our constitutional commentary,"—chiefly, I suggest, because they ask questions which cannot be avoided and which can no more be conclusively answered to everyone's satisfaction than can any other cardinal problem of political philosophy.

The first question that these lectures ask is whether at the time it was adopted the Constitution expressly or impliedly empowered the Court to invalidate action taken by one of the departments within its authority. This is perhaps the easiest inquiry because it is less philosophical than historical. And here I must report that the Judge seems demonstrably in error. The overwhelming view of qualified scholars is that, despite what Judge

Hand asserts, the Eighteenth Century consensus was that the Constitution did give the Court a power to invalidate action which transcended the substantive limitations of the document. A convenient summary of the authorities is in Hart and Wechsler, *The Federal Courts and the Federal System*. A more direct response to Judge Hand's assertion was given in *Toward Neutral Principles of Constitutional Law*, the 1959 Holmes lecture delivered by Professor Herbert Wechsler. Moreover, even if there were better historical grounds for charging the Court with a usurpation, "successful assertion has sealed its title," as Judge Hand himself conceded in 1908. *"Quand tout le monde a tort, tout le monde a raison."* Finally, whatever may have been the intention of the Eighteenth Century framers, the victors in the Civil War who drafted the Thirteenth, Fourteenth, and Fifteenth Amendments and the states which adopted those amendments incontrovertibly intended some federal judicial review of the substance of state legislation.

But to admit that, by original agreement, by subsequent assent, or by appropriate amendment the Court has a judicial veto over the substance of certain legislation, does not settle the question whether the standards set forth in the Bill of Rights are sufficiently specific for judicial enforcement.

Let us concede—for the concession is inevitable—that the phrase "due process" has never achieved, even in. the field of civil liberties, a precise meaning. No Twentieth Century Justice of the Supreme Court has acted on the principle that it is limited to departures from procedural regularity. None has acted on the principle that it is limited to precluding state governments as well as the national government from denying rights specifically. set forth in the Constitution.

Yet such a concession does not require a conclusion that in determining whether a law violates due process the Supreme Court acts entirely at large. What the Court has sought are standards of value which are expressed or implied by the Constitution, which the Court believes are supported by a preponderant, current, and relatively durable public opinion, and which are susceptible of more than a purely subjective assessment. In refusing to accept this approach, Judge Hand takes the position that "values and sacrifices are incommensurables," that the Constitution sets no tables of value, and that the choice made by a legislature must be respected unless the Court is to exercise political powers of a purely legislative character. To me, at least, it seems that Judge Hand ignores essential aspects of American history in assuming that the Constitution does not imply the enforcement of a system of ulterior values with respect to personal liberties. While not set forth in a table of atomic weights, these values and their relative priority are universally recognized as the hallmarks of our society and not an expression of the mere capricious will of individual judges.

> "But value dwells not in particular will;
> It holds his estimate and dignity
> As well wherein 'tis precious of itself
> As in the prizer."

And, despite all the controversy which particular decisions may arouse, there is far more agreement than dispute as to the technique by which to determine whether a particular law has violated the values recognized by the Constitution. On this topic no one has written with greater illumination than Professor Paul A. Freund, particularly in his chapter on "Standards For Civil Liberties" in his masterly volume on *The Supreme Court of* the *United States, Its Business, Purposes and Perform-ance.*

There remains, however, the question whether it is in the interest of democratic government for a bench of judges to exercise a judicial veto over the substance of legislation.

Certainly Professor Thayer's teaching that judicial vetoes undermine civic and legislative responsibility is not a self-evident proposition. On the contrary, the legal presentation of the dominant facts, the forensic canvas of all relevant legal, historical, economic, and social con-siderations, and, above all else, the carefully articulated opinions of judges have nourished public understanding of political issues, increased the care with which laws and ordinances are enacted, and enhanced the role of political theory in political decision. There is hardly a schoolboy whose civic education does not stand in debt to Marshall, Holmes, Brandeis, and other judicial ex-positors of the Constitution.

Nor is it true that respect for law is undermined by dissent. Law is a means of social control, which, while it reflects present power and traditional patterns, is also always open to reconsideration in the light of disinter-ested reason and durable principle. The strength of the law is not in its mystery, but in its capacity to withstand social criticism and intellectual combat. It is the embodi-ment of the Maxim of Heraclitus that "Strife is the source of all things." Obedience to its commands in-creases insofar as their enforcement rests upon persua-sion as well as coercion.

However, we are asked by Judge Hand to realize how far the doctrine of judicial review of legislation will lead to political appointments of judges and to political attacks upon the judicial system. The risk is real. Whoever exercises political power is and ought to be subject to popular criticism, intense, emotional, partisan, and often irrational.

But consider the risks which rejection of the doctrine would entail. Without judicial enforcement, written constitutional declarations of civil liberties are apt to be mere admonitions. Absent an institutionalized framework for their vindication they will have no greater force than the parson's injunction. To be sure, there are countries where the institutionalized framework is supplied by a parliamentary chamber, or a council of revision, or a vigilant press. But our tradition has always emphasized the role of courts in preserving fundamental rights.

Furthermore, in our American experience a fundamental tenet has been that the greatest safeguard for liberty has been the maintenance of multiple centers of power, a built-in series of checks and balances. Under our ever-growing Constitution there has been a prodigious increase in both executive and legislative powers. Today the President has a dominant role in the initiation of domestic and foreign policy. The power of the military establishment, now so clearly intertwined with scientific, technological, and production processes, is unprecedented. A congeries of administrative agencies exercise daily control of myriad activities. The Congress, by virtue of an expanded reading of its powers to tax and to regulate commerce, is master of the whole economic life of the nation, including finance, transport, trade, business, labor, agriculture, and social security. It is against these developments that we should consider the power of the Supreme Court to invalidate legislative and executive action which violates the substantive guarantees of the Constitution. How small, relatively speaking, is that power we are reminded by the perceptive introduction to Eugene V. Rostow's *The Sovereign Prerogative: The Supreme Court and The Quest For Law*. To reduce this relatively small role of the Supreme Court would be greatly to increase the possibilities of executive, legislative, or military tyranny, and could hardly promote the kind of democracy in which the Founding Fathers and Judge Hand were interested.

Nor need we fear that in its exercise of power the Supreme Court will for long act contrary to a durable public opinion. I pass with no more than brief mention the power of Congress to increase the number of justices of the Supreme Court, and its power to regulate the original jurisdiction of the inferior federal courts, and the appellate jurisdiction of all federal courts. What is more significant is that history teaches that the Supreme Court's veto tends not to be so absolute as it is in theory. Whenever Congress has been determined to legislate on a particular subject, it has ultimately prevailed. The judicial veto is in fact a mere suspensive veto, so far as concerns national laws. Regarding local legislation the situation is different. Yet if the Court's decisions on local law produced a strong national reaction, other routes than a Constitutional amendment are available to override the judicial veto. What Congress could do under Section 5 of the Fourteenth Amendment has never been adequately tested. But we do know that widespread protests by state court chief justices and by members of Congress considering legislation restricting the jurisdiction of federal courts have promoted cautious reconsideration of precedents by the Supreme Court.

To summarize, may we not say that while Judge Hand has asked what are undeniably the right and the difficult questions, he has given answers which minimize the practical political ways of maintaining liberty n America, and which reflect to too large an extent his professional view as a high priest in the temple of the law. He is chiefly concerned to keep out of the law avowedly political choices lest at every stage of decision, not merely in constitutional but also in routine cases between the government and the citizen and between private parties, judges come to regard themselves as free of any restrant except to follow their private notions of justice. Such absence of restraint he rightly regards as arbitrary despotism. Nor will any studious observer of the current judicial scene say that Judge Hand's fears are groundless. Judges who daily exercise constitutional power exercise more latitude in cases of statutory construction and of common law rules than do judges whose experience lies in more conventional professional paths. And yet, completely to follow Judge Hand's teachings and to take his strict canons of judicial review, would open, at the present stage of our history, possibilities of political tyranny of far greater dimensions than anything within the scope of judicial caprice.

Unless I am much mistaken, the people of the United States have consciously chosen to adhere to the institution of judicial review because they enjoy a larger measure of democracy within its framework than they would without it. And so long as there are judges with the skepticism, tolerance, and humility of Judge Hand to remind us how cautiously judges should proceed, this popular delegation to the judiciary is not likely to be revoked.

United States District Court
Boston, Massachusetts
March 1963

Contents

I

When a Court Should Intervene

My subject is well-worn; it is not likely that I shall have new light to throw on it; but it is always fresh, and particularly at the present time it is important enough to excuse renewed examination. I shall confine myself to the function of United States courts, particularly the Supreme Court, of declaring invalid statutes of Congress, or of the States, or acts of the President, because they are in conflict with what we have come to call our "Bill of Rights," by which I mean the first eight and the fourteenth amendments of the Constitution of the United States.

As you know Congress proposed the first eight in the same year that the Constitution was ratified, 1789, and they were themselves ratified in 1791. Some of the states had indeed made these amendments a condition upon their ratification of the Constitution, and they were generally regarded as embodying the same political postulates that had been foreshadowed though not fully articulated in the exordium of the Declaration of Independence: "self-evident" and "unalienable rights" with which all men "are endowed by their Creator" and among which are "life, liberty and the pursuit of happiness."

That these were rights arising out of "Natural Laws," "inherent" in the structure of any society, or at least any civilized society, were notions widely accepted at the end of the eighteenth century, and behind them lay a long history, going back to at least the beginning of our era. Even when the powers of king or emperor were at their most absolute and unconditioned peak, it had been conceived that there were limitations valid against any human authority. When the ruler or rulers, be they who they might, exercised powers that went beyond them, their acts were not law at all and nothing could make them so. The easiest support for this attitude was that the source of "Natural Law" was the Will of God; so St. Thomas Aquinas conceived it; so does the Church still assert it; and so did the Deists of the eighteenth century.

It is not my purpose either to assail or to defend this position, nor indeed should I be competent to do so. I shall, however, ask you *arguendo* to assume with me that the Constitution and the "Bill of Rights" neither proceed from, nor have any warrant in, the Divine Will, either as St. Thomas or Jefferson believed; but on the contrary that they are the altogether human expression of the will of the state conventions that ratified them; that their authority depends upon the sanctions available to enforce them; and their meaning is to be gathered from the words they contain, read in the historical setting in which they were uttered. This presupposes that all political power emanates from the people, and that the Constitution distributed among different "Departments" — as Hamilton called them — the authority of each as it was measured by the grant to it. No provision was expressly made, however, as to how a "Department" was to proceed when in the exercise of one of its own powers it became necessary to consider the validity of some earlier act of another "Department." Should the second accept the decision of the first that the act was within the first's authority, or should it decide the question *de novo* according to its own judgment? A third view prevailed, as you all know: that it was a function of the courts to decide which "Department" was right, and that all were bound to accept the decision of the Supreme Court.

The arguments of those who, like Jefferson, held that each "Department" was free to decide the issues before it regardless of how any other "Department" had decided it, was, as I understand it, as follows: The exercise of any delegated power presupposes that the grantee believes that the grant extends to the occasion that has arisen; and it is a necessary incident of the grant itself that he shall so decide before he acts at all. He may of course be wrong; and, when he is, he will be accountable to the grantor; but he is accountable to no one else, unless it be an authority paramount to both himself and the grantor.

The federal courts themselves derive all their powers from the "People of the United States" when they "ordain[ed] and establish[ed]" the Constitution, and the same was true, *ceteris paribus,* of the state courts. One cannot find among the powers granted to courts any authority to pass upon the validity of the decisions of another "Department" as to the scope of that "Department's" powers. Indeed, it is to be understood that the three "Departments" were separate and coequal, each being, as it were, a Leibnizian monad, looking up to the Heaven of the Electorate, but without any mutual dependence. What could be better evidence of complete dependence than to subject the validity of the decision of one "Department" as to its authority on a given occasion to review and reversal by another whose own action was conditioned upon the answer to the same issue? Such a doctrine makes supreme the "Department" that has the last word.

4

Nor can any support for the doctrine of the supremacy of the judiciary be found in the "Supremacy Clause," [1] which, so far as it proves anything, accords rather with the view that, when it was intended to grant courts the power to declare a statute invalid because it was in conflict with the Constitution, some express grant was thought necessary. That clause did indeed require state courts to follow federal laws and the federal constitution when the state laws or the state constitution were "to the contrary"; and that requirement no doubt presupposed that they should have jurisdiction to determine whether a conflict existed. Moreover, we may *arguendo* even admit that when the conflict is between a federal law and a state law or constitution, the state court is to determine the validity of the federal law *quoad* the federal constitution. Furthermore, we may accept Section 25 of the First Judiciary Law as valid, so that on some occasions the Supreme Court might have to decide whether a state court's construction of the Constitution was correct. However, the clause was obviously directed against the states alone to prevent their intruding upon the powers they had delegated or failing to obey limitations on their own powers that they had accepted. Such a grant cannot be stretched into a general authority to pass upon other instances of legislative conflict with the

[1] §2, Article VI.

Constitution; rather we should resort to the maxim, *expressio unius, exclusio alterius,* and declare that it indicates the absence of any such authority.

Before the other side definitively won its way in *Marbury* v. *Madison,*[2] it had been equally vocal, in general as follows. In the first place, it was customary in colonial times for courts to decide whether colonial laws were in accord with colonial charters, and there were several instances after 1776 and before 1787 in which state courts had assumed the same authority as to state statutes. As the Constitution gradually took form in the Convention, again and again in their arguments, members assumed that the federal courts should have the same authority. One of the reasons against a "Council of Revision," of which the Supreme Court was to be a part, was that this would embarrass the exercise of its duty later to determine whether the Constitution had authorized the statute in question. It was the opinion at least of Gerry, Wilson, Mason, Morris, Hamilton, and, although the conclusion appears to me somewhat doubtful, perhaps also of Madison, that the Court was to decide whether a statute was within the powers of Congress. Finally, some decisions of the courts soon after 1789 are inconsistent with any other conclusion. In spite of authority which I am certainly not qualified to

[2] 1 Cranch 137.

6

challenge, I cannot, however, help doubting whether the evidence justifies a certain conclusion that the Convention would have so voted, if the issue had been put to it that courts should have power to invalidate acts of Congress. It is significant that when Hamilton, who, as I have said, and as was in any event to be expected, had apparently been among those who supported the power, came to defend it as he did in the well-known 78th number of the Federalist, he did not suggest that the conclusion followed from anything in the text; but rather from the ordinary function of courts to construe statutes. The following is the meat of his argument:

"It is far more rational to suppose that the courts were designed to be an intermediate body between the people and the legislature in order among other things to keep the latter within the limits assigned to their authority. The interpretation of the laws is the proper and peculiar province of the courts. A constitution is, in fact, and must be regarded by the judges, as a fundamental law. It therefore belongs to them to ascertain its meaning as well as the meaning of any particular act proceeding from the legislative body. . . . Nor does this conclusion by any means suppose a superiority of the judicial to the legislative power. It only supposes that the power of the people is superior to both; and that, where the will of the legislature declared in its statutes

7

stands in opposition to that of the people declared by the Constitution, the judges ought to be governed by the latter rather than the former."

Obviously, Hamilton did not agree with Bishop Hoadley when in a sermon before George the First in 1717 he said: "Whoever hath an absolute authority to interpret written or spoken laws; it is he who is truly the lawgiver to all intents and purposes and not the person who wrote or spoke them."

It is interesting to observe how closely Marshall's reasoning in *Marbury* v. *Madison* [3] followed Hamilton's.

"It is, emphatically, the province and duty of the judicial department, to say what the law is. Those who apply the rule to particular cases, must of necessity expound and interpret that rule. If two laws conflict with each other, the courts must decide on the operation of each. So, if a law be in opposition to the constitution; if both the law and the constitution apply to a particular case, so that the court must either decide that case, conformable to the law, disregarding the constitution; or conformable to the constitution, disregarding the law; the court must determine which of these conflicting rules governs the case; this is of the very essence of judicial duty. If then, the courts are to regard the constitution, and the constitution is superior to any

[3] 1 Cranch 137, 177, 178.

8

ordinary act of the legislature, the constitution, and not such ordinary act, must govern the case to which they both apply."

That reasoning had not always satisfied the Chief Justice, for in *Ware* v. *Hylton*,[4] as counsel for the defendant he had expressed himself as follows:

"The legislative authority of any country can only be restrained by its own municipal constitution; this is a principle that springs from the very nature of society; and the judicial authority can have no right to question the validity of a law, unless such a jurisdiction is expressly given by the constitution. It is not necessary to inquire, how the judicial authority should act, if the legislature were evidently to violate any of the laws of God; but property is the creature of civil society, and subject, in all respects, to the disposition and control of civil institutions."

It is of course true that, when a court decides whether a constitution authorizes a statute, it must first decide what each means, and that, so far, is the kind of duty that courts often exercise, just as they decide conflicts between earlier and later precedents. But if a court, having concluded that a constitution did not authorize the statute, goes on to annul it, its power to do so depends upon an authority that is not involved when only statutes or precedents

[4] 3 Dallas 199, 211.

9

are involved. For a later statute will prevail over an earlier, if they conflict, because a legislature confessedly has authority to change the law as it exists. So too when a court finds two precedents in conflict, it must follow the later one, if that be a decision of a higher court, and it is free to do so if it be one of its own, because, again, confessedly it has authority to change its mind. But when a court declares that a constitution does not authorize a statute, it reviews and reverses an earlier decision of the legislature; and, however well based its authority to do so may be, it does not follow from what it does in the other instances in which the same question does not arise. It does indeed arise when a court is called upon to say whether a statute setting up an administrative tribunal has authorized a regulation of that tribunal. The court has authority to refuse to enforce the regulation if it concludes that the statute did not authorize it, but only because of its conceded power to pass upon the meaning of the statute regardless of how the tribunal may have construed it.

There was nothing in the United States Constitution that gave courts any authority to review the decisions of Congress; and it was a plausible — indeed to my mind an unanswerable — argument that it invaded that "Separation of Powers" which, as so many then believed, was the condition of all free government. That there were other reasons, not only proper but essential, for inferring such a power in the Constitution seems to me certain; but for the moment I am only concerned to show that the reasoning put forward to support the inference will not bear scrutiny.

As an approach, let us try to imagine what would have been the result if the power did not exist. There were two alternatives, each prohibitive, I submit. One was that the decision of the first "Department" before which an issue arose should be conclusive whenever it arose later. That doctrine, coupled with its conceded power over the purse, would have made Congress substantially omnipotent, for by far the greater number of issues that could arise would depend upon its prior action.

Hamilton in the 71st number of the Federalist forecast what would probably have been the result. He was speaking of what he called the "tendency of legislative authority to absorb every other." "In governments purely republican, this tendency is almost irresistible. The representatives of the people in a popular assembly seem sometimes to fancy that they are the people themselves, and betray strong symptoms of impatience and disgust at the least sign of opposition from any other quarter; as if the exercise of its rights by either the executive or the judiciary were a breach of their privilege and an outrage on their dignity. They often appear disposed to exert an imperious control over the other departments; and, as they commonly have the people on their side, they always act with such momentum as to make it very difficult for the other members of the government to maintain the balance of the Constitution."

It was unfair to ascribe to a mere lust for power this disposition of legislators to expand their powers. As Hamilton intimated, every legislator is under constant pressure from groups of constituents whom it does not satisfy to say, "Although I think what you want is right and that you ought to have it, I cannot bring myself to believe that it is within my constitutional powers." Such scruples are not convincing to those whose interests are at stake; and the voters at large will not usually care enough about preserving "the balance of the Constitution" to offset the votes of those whose interests will be disappointed.

The issues that arise are often extremely baffling, and the answers are not obvious. They demand, not only a detached approach, but a training in verbal analysis by no means general among legislators, even though they are usually lawyers. The uncertainties that so often arise are shown by the differences in the answers of the judges themselves. Take for instance the power of Congress to levy taxes in order "to pay the debts and provide for the common defense and general Welfare of the United States."

There is indeed no great difficulty in deciding whether a tax is "to pay the debts" of the United States; but at times it is hard to say whether a statute is a tax to "provide for the . . . general Welfare." An excise might be in form a tax and yet not raise enough revenue to pay for the cost of its administration. Furthermore, is the taxing power limited to raising money necessary to the exercise of some of the prescribed powers of Congress, or does it extend to whatever Congress may think beneficial to the "People"?

Again, consider the power "to regulate commerce with foreign nations and among the several States." Are all "regulations" valid so long as they impinge only upon "commerce among the States"? It is constitutional to prevent those who do not pay a minimum wage, or who employ child labor, from sending their wares across state lines; but would it be constitutional to forbid carpenters, plumbers, bakers, or brewers to do so, unless they passed a federal examination and received a federal license? Do the natural resources in land under water below low tide belong to the nation or the abutting states?

What I have called the first alternative would have meant that the interpretation of the Constitution on a given occasion would be left to that "Department" before which the question happened first to come; and such a system would have been so capricious in operation, and so different from that designed, that it could not have endured. Moreover, the second alternative would have been even worse, for under it each "Department" would have been free to decide constitutional issues as it thought right, regardless of any earlier decision of the others. Thus it would have been the President's privilege, and indeed his duty, to execute only those statutes that seemed to him to be constitutional, regardless even of a decision of the Supreme Court. The courts would have entered such judgments as seemed to them consonant with the Constitution; but neither the President, nor Congress, would have been bound to enforce them if he or it disagreed, and without their help the judgments would have been waste paper.

For centuries it has been an accepted canon in interpretation of documents to interpolate into the text such provisions, though not expressed, as are essential to prevent the defeat of the venture at hand; and this applies with especial force to the interpretation of constitutions, which, since they are designed to cover a great multitude of necessarily unforeseen occasions, must be cast in general language, unless they are constantly amended. If so, it was altogether in keeping with established practice for the Supreme Court to assume an authority to keep the states, Congress, and the President within their prescribed powers. Otherwise the government could not proceed as planned; and indeed would almost certainly have foundered, as in fact it almost did over that very issue.

However, since this power is not a logical deduction from the structure of the Constitution but only a practical condition upon its successful operation, it need not be exercised whenever a court sees, or thinks that it sees, an invasion of the Constitution. It is always a preliminary question how importunately the occasion demands an answer. It may be better to leave the issue to be worked out without authoritative solution; or perhaps the only solution available is one that the court has no adequate means to enforce. As we all know, the Supreme Court has steadfastly refused to decide constitutional issues that it deems to involve "political questions" — a term it has never tried to define — although this feature of the doctrine has been a stench in the nostrils of strict constructionists. "If the courts have authority to intervene at all, by what warrant," these ask, "do they determine to use, or to withhold it, at their pleasure? Who made them the arbiters of all political authority in the nation with a discretion to act or not, as they please?

Is this a government of law, as we have always supposed, or in the end only one of men?"

I shall not try to enumerate all the occasions when the Court has stood aloof, but these are a few. The United States expressly guarantees to every state "a Republican Form of Government," [5] but the Court will not determine whether an amendment to a state constitution has made it no longer "Republican." Section two of the Fourteenth Amendment requires that "representatives shall be apportioned among the several States according to their respective numbers," but the Court will not decide whether they have been properly apportioned.

Nor will it consider whether a state legislature has ratified a federal constitutional amendment, as required by Article V, if Congress chooses to accept the return of the state officials as true. If the Speaker of the House and the Vice-President both so declare by signing a bill, the Court will not inquire whether it is in the same terms as the documents on which the House and Senate voted. It will not inquire whether, contrary to the official return, the number of legislators required by a state constitution have in fact voted for a bill.

It is true that the Court has never said that it would not decide whether an "executive agree-

[5] §14, Article IV.

ment" of the President with another nation was a "treaty," which requires the "advice and consent of the Senate"; but it has several times affirmed the validity of such agreements that one cannot help thinking were treaties in all but form, and its language has seemed to imply that the President's decision is final. It will not decide whether the governor of one state has lawfully refused to deliver up a fugitive charged with crime upon another governor's requisition though the language of the Constitution seems imperative.[6] There are no "coercive means to compel" performance of the duty.

Finally, consider President Eisenhower's ruling as to what evidence officers of the Army may be required to give at hearings of a sub-committee of the Senate. The support of this, as I understand it, was that the President, as a corollary of his prerogatives as Commander-in-Chief, had the constitutional authority to decide what evidence the Army should disclose. There have been a number of other occasions when Presidents have refused similar demands, yet is it not possible to argue that Congress, especially now that the appropriations for the armed forces are the largest items of the budget, should be allowed to inquire in as much detail as it wishes, not only how past appropriations have in fact been spent, but in general about the conduct of the

[6] §2 (2) Article IV.

national defense? Nevertheless, would you not, like me, guess that the Court would refuse to pass on the controversy?

Thus we are brought to the historical justification that I mentioned a few moments ago for interpolating as a gloss upon the Constitution the authority of courts to assert their primacy as interpreters of the authority of other "Departments," which are, in theory anyway, coordinate and equal with themselves. In particular, what justification is there for imputing such an authority when it rests at best only upon implication, and when its exercise, if "political questions" are to be answered, rests in the discretion of the putative interpreters?

May I start with some words of my unforgettable master, John Chipman Gray, in his Columbia Lectures on the "Nature and Sources of the Law"? "The difficulties of so-called interpretation arise when the legislature has no meaning at all; when the question which is raised on the statute never occurred to it; when what the judges have to do is, not to determine what the legislature did mean on a point that was not present to its mind, but to guess what it would have intended on a point not present to its mind, had the point been present." [7] I cannot believe that any of us would say that the "meaning" of an utterance is exhausted by the spe-

[7] Gray, *Nature and Sources of the Law,* §370.

cific content of the utterer's mind at the moment. Do you not all agree with Holmes, J., in repudiating that position which he described as follows: "We see what you are driving at, but you have not said it, and therefore we shall go on as before." [8]

What does a body of men like a legislature "mean" by the words contained in a statute? What "points" are "present" to their minds? Indeed what "points" were common in the minds of a majority of those who voted? These are unanswerable questions. All we know is that a majority has accepted the sequence of words in which the "law" has been couched, and that they expect the judges to decide whether an occasion before them is one of those that the words cover. That is an intricate process made up of many factors; perhaps the single most important one is the general purpose, declared in, or to be imputed to, the command. Gray calls the result a "guess" and indeed it is; but who are we that we should insist upon certainties in a world of no more at best than probabilities? May I break from its setting an epigram of my friend, Bernard Berenson: "In the beginning was the Guess"? Yes, my friends, in the beginning and at the ending let us be content with the "Guess." What we do, and what we must do, when the text baffles us is nowhere better expressed than by Plowden in the much-quoted note

[8] *Johnson* v. *United States,* 163 Fed. 30, 32.

to *Eyston* v. *Studd*,[9] which I ask your indulgence
to repeat in part:

"In order to form a right judgment when the
letter of a statute is restrained, and when enlarged
by equity, it is a good way, when you peruse a
statute, to suppose that the law-maker is present,
and that you have passed him the question you want
to know touching the equity, then you must give
yourself such an answer as you may imagine he
would have done, if he had been present. As for
example, . . . where the strangers scale the walls,
and defend the city, suppose the law-maker to be
present with you, and in your mind put this question to him, shall the strangers be put to death?
Then give yourself the same answer which you
imagine he, being an upright and reasonable man,
would have given, and you will find that he would
have said 'They shall not be put to death.' . . . And
therefore when such cases happen which are within
the letter, or out of the letter, of a statute, and yet
don't directly fall within the plain and natural pur-
port of the letter, but are in some measure to be
conceived in a different idea from that in which the
text seems to express, it is a good way to give questions
and give answers to yourself thereupon, in the same
manner as if you were actually conversing with the
maker of such laws, and by this means you will easily

[9] 2 Plowden 459, 467.

find out what is the equity of those cases. And if the law-maker would have followed the equity, notwithstanding the words of the law (as Aristotle says he would, for he says, quod etiam legislator, si adesset, admoneret, etiamsi jam legem tulisset) you may safely do the like, for while you do no more than the law-maker would have done, you do not act contrary to the law, but in conformity to it."

As for the passage from Aristotle that he cites it is this:

"All law is universal but about some things it is not possible to make a universal statement which shall be correct. In those cases then in which it is necessary to speak universally but not possible to do so correctly, the law takes the usual case, though it is not ignorant of the possibility of error. And it is none the less correct; for the error is not in the law nor in the legislator but in the nature of the thing, since the matter of practical affairs is of this kind from the start. When the law speaks universally, then, and a case arises on it which is not covered by the universal statement, then it is right, where the legislator fails us and has erred by oversimplicity, to correct the omission — to say what the legislator himself would have put into his law, if he had known. Hence the equitable is just, and better than one kind of justice — not better than absolute justice but better than the error that arises from the absoluteness of the statement. And this is the nature of the equitable, a correction of law where it is defective owing to its universality. In fact this is the reason why all things are not determined by law, viz, that about some things it is impossible to lay down a law, so that a decree is needed." [10]

And if you are not too averse to more Aristotle, maybe this will also help to pave my way:

"We saw that there are two kinds of right and wrong conduct towards others, one provided by written ordinances, the other by unwritten. We have now discussed the kind about which the laws have something to say. The other kind has itself two varieties. . . . The second kind makes up for a community's written code of law. Its existence partly is, and partly is not, intended by legislators; not intended, where they find themselves unable to define things exactly, and are obliged to legislate as if that held good always which in fact only holds good usually; or where it is not easy to be complete, owing to the endless possible cases presented, such as the kinds and sizes of weapons that may be used to inflict wounds — a lifetime would be too short to make out a complete list of these. If, then, a precise statement is impossible and yet legislation is necessary, the law must be expressed in wide

[10] Ethics, Book V, Chapter 10 fol. 1137, lines 12–28.

terms; and so, if a man has no more than a finger-ring on his hand when he lifts to strike, or actually strikes, another man, he is guilty of a criminal act according to the written words of the law; but he is innocent really, and it is equity that declares him to be so." [11]

In other words a law couched in general terms *prima facie* includes all occasions that the words cover, and therefore presupposes a choice on each occasion between some value to be attained and some sacrifice to be accepted. It assumes that its advance appraisal of each value and sacrifice in this equation will not vary too much from the later appraisal. This assumption is not trouble-some, so far as the values and sacrifices do not vary in the different settings in which they appear, but they do vary greatly, so that an occasion may arise that, although it is within the words used, imposes a choice between values and sacrifices altogether different from any that the legislators would have made if they could have foreseen the occasion.

There are two ways of meeting this difficulty. A statute may rigidly declare those specific occasions to which it will apply, making it plain that it means to cover all occasions within the lexicographic scope of the words and no others. Although that will not indeed avoid all doubts, it will do so in proportion

11 Rhetoric, Book 1, Chapter 13, fol. 1374, lines 18–40.

as the language is specific, as for example, when a coined vocabulary is used. It is seldom, however, that the purpose behind a statute is so limited that it is possible in advance to imagine all the occasions which the legislators would wish to include, if they had thought of them.

The other way is to leave the proliferation of the purpose to those who are to be entrusted with effecting it; the "interpreters." This too has its defects, it involves an imaginative projection of the minds of those who uttered the words that in Gray's words can be no better than a "guess," and, as you may recall, he believes that it is usually only a cover for the substitution of the "interpreter's" personal choice, even though it be determined by what he may conceive to be the "principles of morality." (Incidentally, it is not apparent to me why it should be supposed that an "interpreter," if he tries to give the "principles of morality" an objective meaning other than his personal preference, will be more successful than when he tries to imagine how the authors of the statute would have dealt with the occasion.)

However, be the difficulties what they may, there can be no doubt that this second way is that adopted in countless instances in the administration of mature jural systems. Indeed we have carried it so far in the interpretation of statutes that at times in order to effect the obvious design we have actually disregarded words or phrases whose scope admitted of no doubt, and that stood flatly in the path of the reading adopted.[12] A classic paradigm is the supposed acquittal of a surgeon who might bleed a patient contrary to the express prohibition of the statute against drawing blood in the streets of Bologna. Much of the law of torts, including the law of negligence, is based upon just this kind of delegation of an authority, leaving to the "interpreter" the appraisal of the conflicting interests on which the jural choice is to depend.

"Reasonable care" — that latchkey to so many legal doors — is the care that a "reasonable man" would exercise on the occasion in question. And who is this "reasonable man"? Let me answer in the words of the American Law Institute: he is "a person exercising those qualities of attention, knowledge, intelligence and judgment which society requires of its members for the protection of their own interests and the interests of others." [13] Let me again draw from the same source. The proper question to put to oneself in such cases is "whether the magnitude of the risk outweighs the value which the law attaches to the conduct which involves it." [14] Once

[12] *United States* v. *Kirby,* 7 Wall. 482, 486; *Holy Trinity Church* v. *United States,* 143 U.S. 457; *Markam* v. *Cabell,* 326 U.S. 404, 407.
[13] Torts §283 (a).   [14] Torts §283 (c).

more: "The standard to which the actor must conform is that of a reasonably careful person under like circumstances; in other words that which is customarily regarded as requisite for the protection of others rather than that of the average man in the community. The two are generally identical, but, occasionally, the actor in particular situations is required to exercise an attention which is far higher than that which is exercised by any but a few members of the community." [15] That is, the public may condemn its own customary carelessness.

The duties of fiduciaries: trustees, agents, corporate directors and the rest; and of bona fide purchasers and the creditors of insolvents, are, as you know, left at large, to be measured in each case by what can only be deemed an authentic bit of special legislation. Consider also that test for citizenship that the alien shall have been a person of "good moral character" during the preceding five years; or the test of deportation that the alien shall not have been twice convicted of crimes "involving moral turpitude." Finally, think of this matchless instance; the test laid down of what is "restraint of trade" under the Anti-Trust Acts. Here is what passed for a definition:

"Applying the rule of reason to the construction of the statute, it was held in the Standard Oil Case

[15] Torts §289 (i).

2 6

that as the words 'restraint of trade' at common law and in the law of this country at the time of the adoption of the Anti-trust Act only embraced acts or contracts or agreements or combinations which operated to the prejudice of the public interests by unduly restricting competition or unduly obstructing the due course of trade or which, either because of their inherent nature or effect or because of the evident purpose of the acts, etc., injuriously restrained trade, that the words as used in the statute were designed to have and did have but a like significance. It was therefore pointed out that the statute did not forbid or restrain the power to make normal and usual contracts to further trade by resorting to all normal methods." [16]

Let me sum up what I have tried to say. My first conclusion is that, when the Constitution emerged from the Convention in September, 1787, the structure of the proposed government, if one looked to the text, gave no ground for inferring that the decisions of the Supreme Court, and *a fortiori* of the lower courts, were to be authoritative upon the Executive and the Legislature. Each of the three "Departments" was an agency of a sovereign, the "People of the United States." Each was responsible to that sovereign, but not to one another; indeed, their "Separation" was still regarded as a condition of free

[16] *United States* v. *American Tobacco Co.*, 221 U.S. 106, 179

government, whatever we may think of that notion now. Moreover, it is impossible to have any assurance how the Convention would have voted at the time, had the question been put to it whether the Supreme Court should have a conclusive authority to construe the Constitution. Although this was the opinion of a number of the most influential members, the issue was highly controversial, and there can be no certainty what would have been the outcome of a vote. True, under the "Supremacy Clause" state courts would at times have to decide whether state laws and constitutions, or even a federal statute, were in conflict with the federal constitution; but the fact that this jurisdiction was confined to such occasions, and that it was thought necessary specifically to provide such a limited jurisdiction, looks rather against than in favor of a general jurisdiction. The arguments deducing the court's authority from the structure of the new government, or from the implications of any government, were not valid, in spite of the deservedly revered names of their authors. Although they rightly declared that it was the province of the courts to construe the meaning of statutes, and, when they conflict, to determine which shall prevail, they did not observe that a conflict between a statute and a constitution raises a question not present in deciding a conflict between an earlier and a later statute. In the first situation the court ose frontiers. The doctrine presupposed that it as possible to make such a distinction, though at mes it is difficult to do so. What I shall have to say ereafter will be no more than a discussion of how his distinction can be observed in applying the prohibitions in the First, Fifth, and Fourteenth Amendments, cast as these are in such sweeping terms that their history does not elucidate their contents.

that annuls the statute must reverse a pr{...}
cision of the legislature that there was n{...}
in the second, the existence of a conflict is i{...}
because the legislature is not bound by it{...}
statute.

On the other hand it was probable, if i{...}
was not certain, that without some arbiter{...}
decision should be final the whole system{...}
have collapsed, for it was extremely unlikel{...}
the Executive or the Legislature, having on{...}
cided, would yield to the contrary holding of an{...}
"Department," even of the courts. The courts{...}
undoubtedly the best "Department" in which to{...}
such a power, since by the independence of t{...}
tenure they were least likely to be influenced{...}
diverting pressure. It was not a lawless act to imp{...}
into the Constitution such a grant of power. On t{...}
contrary, in construing written documents it h{...}
always been thought proper to engraft upon the te{...}
such provisions as are necessary to prevent the fa{...}
ure of the undertaking. That is no doubt a dang{...}
ous liberty, not lightly to be resorted to; but it w{...}
justified in this instance, for the need was comp{...}
ling. On the other hand it was absolutely essenti{...}
to confine the power to the need that evoked it: th{...}
is, it was and always has been necessary to distingui{...}
between the frontiers of another "Department'{...}
authority and the propriety of its choices withi{...}

II

The Fifth and Fourteenth
Amendments

In my last lecture I based the power of a court to hold a statute invalid upon the necessity in such a system as ours of some authority whose word should be final as to when another "Department" had overstepped the borders of its authority. On the other hand it is quite as important that within its prescribed borders each "Department" and the states shall be free from interference.

My topic being the "Bill of Rights," by which, as I have said, I mean the first eight and the fourteenth amendments, I am not concerned with those decisions that have marked the division between the powers of the nation and of the states, for the "Bill of Rights" is concerned only with the protection of the individual against the impact of federal or state law. There is one doctrine, however, that, although it is irrelevant to the "Bill of Rights," so well discloses the kind of *media concludendi* used in constitutional cases that it justifies a short digression. I mean the doctrine established in *Gibbons* v. *Ogden*,[17] that the grant of power to regulate interstate commerce (§8 [3] Art. I) deprived the states of legislative jurisdiction over such commerce even in the absence of any "regulation" by Congress. With this doctrine, Taney, Kent, and a good many others did not agree; and perhaps it was never true in quite the stark form that I have just stated it; nor shall I venture a guess as to how much of it still remains. Indeed, as an isolated issue it is hard to see why Congress's power by statute to regulate interstate commerce was not adequate to accomplish the purpose of the clause, because no matter what the states might enact, it could substitute whatever "regulation" it thought necessary to restore the proper balance between states and nation. Meanwhile, so long as Congress chose not to intervene there would be at least some sort of supervision over interstate transactions.

Yet at times I have asked myself whether the following considerations were not a justification, at least at the beginning, for such an extreme construction of the clause. The states were extremely jealous of all federal power and long remained so; they more or less associated it with the centralized and

[17] 9 Wheat. 1.

remote government against which they had rebelled. We are apt now to forget this and to think of their hostility as confined to slavery; we do not recall how widely it pervaded the whole nation, and extended to all kinds of legislation. Therefore, I suggest that it was not altogether irrational for Marshall and the Court to ask themselves whether, if "commerce among the states" were left open to state regulation, there might not arise such a tangle of conflicts as would tend not only to strain the whole national fabric, but to impede the eventual assertion of the power of Congress because of the vested interests that might have grown up. The important thing was to have an authority that would finally put an end to the rivalries that might arise by submitting them to a single authority *ab initio*.

After this excursion into matters not relevant to my subject let me turn to the limitations upon all governmental authority contained in the amendments that I have mentioned. It is theoretically possible to construe these prohibitions in one of three ways. First, we may read them as embodying the limitations that were current in 1787, and so through their history to give them a more or less definite content. Second, we may read them in the Jeffersonian or Thomistic idiom as postulates embodying the "unalienable rights" with which men "are endowed by their Creator"; or, if we prefer the locution, as part of "Natural Law." As such they become imperative, *semper ut ubique,* upon Legislatures, Executives, and Courts. There are many who do profess so to understand them, but, as I have already said, I am assuming there are no such postulates accessible to courts. Third, we may read them as admonitory or hortatory, not definite enough to be guides on concrete occasions, prescribing no more than that temper of detachment, impartiality, and an absence of self-directed bias that is the whole content of justice: *constans et perpetua voluntas suum cuique tribunendi.* So regarded, it is, however, impossible to apply to these clauses the canon that I have quoted from Plowden and that he borrowed from Aristotle. Not that they are not commands, for indubitably they are; but it would be fatuous to attempt imaginatively to concoct how the Founding Fathers would have applied them to the regulation of a modern society. Not only is it true that, "if by the statement that what the Constitution meant at the time of its adoption is what it means to-day it is intended to say that the great clauses of the Constitution must be confined to the interpretation which the framers, with the conditions and outlook of their time, would have placed upon them, the statement carries its own refutation";[18] but it is also impossible to fab-

[18] *Home Building and Loan Association* v. *Blaisdell,* 290 U.S. 398, 443.

ricate how the "Framers" would have answered the problems that arise in a modern society had they been reared in the civilization that has produced those problems. We should indeed have to be sorcerers to conjure up how they would have responded.

It is my understanding that the "Due Process Clause," when it first appeared in Chapter III of the 28th of Edward III — about a century and a half after Magna Carta — was a substitute for, and was regarded as the equivalent of, the phrase, *per legem terrae,* which meant no more than customary legal procedure. I believe that it had never been construed otherwise before Coke's gloss upon it in Bonham's case, which did say that "when an Act of Parliament is against common right and reason, or repugnant, or impossible to be performed, the common law will control it and adjudge such Act to be void." [19]

There can be little doubt that this was an extension to statutes of the doctrine that, as I have said, had always hovered in the minds even of English lawyers of an implicit limitation upon all regal power. However, as to Parliament it never took root in English law in which, as you know, once their meaning has been ascertained, statutes have always been unconditionally imperative. In 1856 the Supreme Court in *Murray's Lessee* v. *Hoboken Land*

[19] 8 Rep. 118a.

and Improvement Co.[20] spoke as though the clause touched only those customary legal steps that were necessary to invoke forcible sanctions. The question was whether a sale of property for unpaid taxes was valid, though made without notice to the taxpayer, or without any adversary hearing; and the decision was put upon the ground that "we must look to those settled usages and modes of proceeding existing in the common and statute law of England before the emigration of our ancestors and which are shown not to have been unsuited to their civil and political condition by having been acted on after the settlement of this country." However, in 1857 in *Dred Scott* v. *Sandford*,[21] Taney, C.J., in the following passage of his opinion, interpreted the clause as a limit upon the power of Congress to confiscate property rights, regardless of the procedure prescribed:

"Thus the rights of property are united with the rights of person, and placed on the same ground by the Fifth Amendment to the Consitution, which provides that no person shall be deprived of life, liberty, and property, without due process of law. And an Act of Congress which deprives a citizen of the United States of his liberty or property, merely because he came himself or brought his property into a particular Territory of the United States, and

[20] 18 How. 272, 277.   [21] 19 How. 393, 450.

3 6

who had committed no offence against the laws, could hardly be dignified with the name of due process of law."

That decision, it is true, was not a propitious harbinger for an extension of the doctrine; but, as everyone knows, the Clause soon became regarded as covering substantial, as well as procedural rights, and that has now become its paramount importance.

The test of the proper scope of judicial review of a statute being, as I have said, only to set the ambit of what is legislation and not to redress any abuses in the exercise of power, one cannot escape the task of finding what are its constituent factors — a hazardous duty. First, I fancy that all will agree that the existing status quo must have occasioned discontent. To set matters right the legislature must therefore first understand the facts as they are, and follow this by some sort of prophetic forecast of the effect of the measure proposed.

Both these inquiries are difficult, especially the second; for not only is it substantially impossible to forecast the remoter results of any social readjustment, but it is even more difficult to know how far the command will be obeyed. However, difficult as both these undertakings are, they are relatively simple compared with deciding whether the proposed change will be beneficial to the society on which it is imposed. That presupposes a choice and all choices depend upon an appraisal of the values and sacrifices to which the contemplated action will give rise. Values and sacrifices are incommensurables, not being made up of elements common to each other, unless they are themselves composite — which only multiplies the difficulty. Each carries its own charge of satisfaction or dissatisfaction, which usually varies with its setting, so that the same object may give one degree of gratification or discontent at one time, and a different degree at another. We say that we "weigh" our joys and sorrows when we choose between them, but that is a metaphor expressing our sense of inner tension, for choice, at least in the universe of desire, is as immediate, absolute and underived as are its component values and sacrifices. Our lives are successful only in proportion as we correctly forecast at the time of choice how we shall feel if the choice is realized. All this becomes incredibly more difficult when we are forced to choose for others, especially for large groups, for these are made up of individuals, each having his own scale of values, and practically we can proceed at all only by assuming that the differences will cancel out enough to be disregarded, or by contriving a vicarious substitute, to which we impute values and sacrifices that we believe to be as little alien as possible to those current at the time. This is what courts do on their own initiative in those of the public require but what measures are necessary for the protection of such interests."

He then went on to describe as follows what were the conditions upon the court's exercise of its veto. It must appear, "first, that the interests of the public generally, as distinguished from those of a particular class, require such interference; and, second, that the means are reasonably necessary for the accomplishment of the purpose, and not unduly oppressive upon individuals. The legislature may not, under the guise of protecting the public interests, arbitrarily interfere with private business, or impose unusual and unnecessary restrictions upon lawful occupations. In other words, its determination as to what is a proper exercise of its police powers is not final or conclusive, but is subject to the supervision of the courts."

Such a definition leaves no alternative to regarding the court as a third legislative chamber. When is it "arbitrary" to interfere with private business in order to protect "the public interests"? What are "unnecessary restrictions upon lawful occupations"? What is "a proper exercise of the police power" and what "supervision" are the courts to have of its exercise? In retrospect it is indeed amazing that such a patent usurpation should have remained unchallenged for as long as it did. In the end what had in fact happened did indeed begin to transpire, and

many situations that I spoke of in my first lecture, when we hide our incapacity to dispose of a future controversy by deputing it to the putative choice of that factitious ghost, the "reasonable man."

However, if what I have said is true of those choices that any statute imposes, I do not see how a court can invalidate them without putting itself in the same position and declaring whether the legislature's substitute is what the court would have coined to meet the occasion. True, courts might, and indeed they always do, disclaim authority to intervene unless they are sure beyond doubt that the compromise imposed is wrong; but that does not disguise the fact that their choice is an authentic exercise of the same process that produced the statute itself. On the other hand, if a court goes so far as that, surely it may not say that it is doing no more than keeping a legislature within its accredited authority, and that it is not assuming power itself to review the legislative choice *de novo*. How would it do then to avoid this antinomy by saying that the limits of a legislature's power are determined by the rightness of the adjustments it prescribes between the conflicting values and sacrifices before it? Why not exclude as not legislative at all any compromises that are too flagrantly wrong? In accord with some such vague principle it seems to have satisfied judicial scruples for a season to say that the extent of legislative authority was measured by that curiously inept phrase, the "Police Power."

By whom and where the term was first used I do not know; but it appears in substance in other connections in 1827,[22] 1837,[23] and 1847,[24] and in the opinions of the state courts in 1851 [25] and 1856.[26] For example, in "The License Cases," Taney, C. J., described it in the following words as a means of marking the bounds of interstate commerce: "What are the police powers of a state? They are nothing more nor less than the powers of government inherent in every sovereignty to the extent of its dominions. And whether a State passes a quarantine law, or a law to punish offences, or to establish courts of justice, or requiring certain instruments to be recorded or to regulate commerce within its limits, in every case it exercises the same powers, that is to say, the power of sovereignty, the power to govern men and things within the limits of its dominions." Obviously those words did not define any part of legislative power but included all of it.

Again in "The Slaughter-House Cases," [27] Miller, J., spoke of the "Police Power" in substantially the

[22] *Brown* v. *Maryland,* 12 Wheat. 419, 443.
[23] *New York* v. *Miln,* 11 Peters 102, 141.
[24] The License Cases, 5 How. 504, 583.
[25] *Commonwealth* v. *Alger,* 7 Cushing 53, 85.
[26] *Wynhamer* v. *People,* 13 N.Y. 378, 452.
[27] 16 Wall. 36, 62.

same way: "This power is and must be from its v nature, incapable of any very exact definition limitation. Upon it depends the security of the soc order, the life and health of the citizens, the co fort of an existence in a thickly settled communi the enjoyment of private and social life and beneficial use of property."

Since, so defined, the "Power" embraced all co promises, adjustments and compositions of any ki whatever, if the "Due Process Clause" was not invade the sphere of legislation the "Power" m have clearer outlines. There were a good many forts to find satisfactory definitions that would bounds to it, but, as might have been expected, th all ended in failure. As good an effort as any w that of Justice Brown in 1894 in *Lawton* v. *Steele* He was discussing a state statute that made it lawf to confiscate the nets and other tackle of fisherm who invaded a state's waters, in the course of whi he declared that the power would "include eve thing essential to public safety, health and moral He enumerated a number of examples of the prop exercise of the power, which did not however haust the list, because "the State may interfere whe ever the public interests demand it and in this p ticular a large discretion is necessarily vested in legislature to determine, not only what the intere

[28] 152 U.S. 133, 156, 157.

with the increasing demand for social regulation resentment began to mount. By 1912 this had grown so formidable as to produce the doctrine of the "Recall of Judicial Decisions," which had a large — probably a determinative — part in the rise of the Progressive Party and the defeat of the Republican Party after a control of over fifty years, broken only by the two terms of President Cleveland.

Nevertheless, the underlying notion continued in spite of continually increasing exceptions; and apparently it has not even yet wholly disappeared even as to economic interests. The decision of a bare majority in 1934 that a state may fix the price of milk [29] was taken by some people as a *coup de grace* of the old doctrine, though it really should not have been so taken, as appeared from the following consolatory saving placebos. "The guaranty of due process, as has often been held, demands only that the law shall not be unreasonable, arbitrary or capricious, and the means selected shall have a real and substantial relation to the object sought to be attained" (p. 525). Again: "If the laws passed are seen to have reasonable relation to a proper legislative purpose and are neither arbitrary nor discriminatory, the requirements of due process are satisfied" (p. 537). And this: "Price control, like any other form of regulation, is unconstitutional only if arbitrary,

[29] *Nebbia* v. *New York,* 291 U.S. 502.

discriminatory, or demonstrably irrelevant to the policy the legislature is free to adopt, and hence an unnecessary and unwarranted interference with individual liberty" (p. 539).

It is hard to read this language as more than a decent burial salute after the following language appeared eighteen years later: "Our recent decisions make plain that we do not sit as a superlegislature to weigh the wisdom of legislation, nor to decide whether the policy which it expresses offends the public welfare. The legislative power has limits, as *Tot* v. *United States,* 319 U.S. 463 holds. But the state legislatures have constitutional authority to experiment with new techniques: they are entitled to their own standard of the public welfare; they may within extremely broad limits control practices in the business-labor field, so long as specific constitutional prohibitions are not violated and so long as conflicts with valid and controlling federal laws are avoided." [30]

Or this: "The day is gone when this court uses the Due Process Clause of the Fourteenth Amendment to strike down state laws regulatory of business and industrial conditions, because they are improvident, or out of harmony with a particular school of thought." [31] It remained indeed true that procedur-

[30] *Day-Brite Lighting, Inc.* v. *Missouri,* 342 U.S. 421, 423.
[31] *Williamson* v. *Lee Optical Co.,* 348 U.S. 483, 488.

ally the owner of property still had the protection of adequate notice and an opportunity to present his own evidence, and to be presented with his adversary's; and the same is true of less tangible interests;[32] but for these there was a background of precedent which has always been recognized as interpretative.

One would suppose that these decisions and the opinions that accompanied them had put an end — at least when economic interests only were at stake — to any judicial review of a statute because the choice made between the values and sacrifices in conflict did not commend itself to the court's notions of justice. That would, however, be too hasty a conclusion because in one of its most recent decisions the Court did intervene [33] and annulled a state statute for just such reasons. It is true that this was by virtue of the "Equal Protection Clause," but the language used applied as well to the "Due Process Clause." "Of course, distinctions in the treatment of business entities engaged in the same business activity may be justified by genuinely different characteristics of the business involved. This is so even where distinction is by name. But distinctions cannot be so justified if the 'discrimination has no reasonable relation to those differences.' "

[32] *Anti-Fascist Committee* v. *McGrath*, 341 U.S. 123.
[33] *Morey* v. *Doud*, 354 U.S. 457, 466, 469.

Again, "[T]aking all of these factors in conjunction — the remote relationship of the statutory classification to the Act's purpose or to business characteristics, and the creation of a closed class by the singling out of the money orders of a named company, with accompanying economic advantages — we hold that the application of the Act to appellees deprives them of equal protection of the laws."

I trust it is not disrespectful to say that I find it impossible to predict what attitude the Court would take towards a statute of which it much disapproved even where it concerned economic issues only; and as will appear, the answer becomes decidedly more obscure when the statute touches those other interests, now called "Personal Rights." In theory an escape would always be possible if courts were free to scrutinize the motives of the legislators who have voted for a statute; but of all conceivable issues this would be the most completely "political," and no court would undertake it.[34] That has been the uniform ruling whenever the question has arisen, nowhere stated more uncompromisingly than by Taney, C. J., in the following passages from his opinion in "The License Cases":

[34] *McCulloch* v. *Maryland*, 4 Wheat. 316, 423; *Doyle* v. *Continental Ins. Co.*, 94 U.S. 535, 541; *Weber* v. *Freed*, 239 U.S. 325, 330; *Arizona* v. *California*, 283 U.S. 423, 435; *Daniel* v. *Family Insurance Co.*, 336 U.S. 220, 224.

"Upon that question the object and motive of the States are of no importance, and cannot influence the decision. It is a question of power. Are the States absolutely prohibited by the Constitution from making any regulations of foreign commerce? If they are, then such regulations are null and void, whatever be the motive of the State or whatever the real object of the law." [35]

A different situation does arise when the grant of legislative authority is itself specifically conditioned, as for example in the case of the powers of Congress, granted by §8 of Article I of the Constitution. Apparently the test of whether a power has been exceeded may then be the legislative purpose. So far as I know the decisions have all arisen under tax statutes, which sometimes disclose their purpose from their inevitable effect. We may start with a conceivable occasion when everyone must agree that the statute could not possibly raise any net revenue, and yet it must be a tax to be valid at all: for example, suppose an excise tax of $50 an ounce upon the sale of potable alcohol. At the other extreme are those statutes that, although they levy taxes that will bring in a net revenue, have an added and incidental purpose. Indeed it is hard to imagine any tax whose imposition was not in some degree dictated by its effect upon the public interest, and that

[35] 5 How. 504, 582.

has uniformly been held to be irrelevant.[36] But there is a third group which the Court held not to come within any other power defined in section 8 of Article I than the power "to lay and collect taxes" and which did lay taxes that apparently would produce a net revenue, but were nevertheless unconstitutional because that was in no sense any part of their purpose.[37]

Last are those decisions that hold a statute invalid, not because the command is contrary to anything in the Constitution, but because some other authority, usually an administrative tribunal, has been given jurisdiction over the dispute. This is a different situation from one when the language of the command is not definite enough to be intelligible; for, when that is so, the statute is not indeed unconstitutional but is not a statute at all; because a command must be understandable to those to whom it is addressed. Gray says, if I understand him, that, no matter how obscure the text, a judge is not "justified in refusing to pass on a controversy because there is no person or book or custom to tell him how to decide it. He must find out for himself; he must determine what

36 *Veazie Bank* v. *Fenno,* 8 Wall. 533, 548; *McCray* v. *United States,* 195 U.S. 27, 64; *United States* v. *Doremus,* 249 U.S. 86; *Sonzinsky* v. *United States,* 300 U.S. 506, 514; *United States* v. *Kahriger,* 345 U.S. 22, 28.

37 *The Child Labor Tax Case,* 259 U.S. 20, 37; *Hill* v. *Wallace,* 259 U.S. 44, 66; *United States* v. *Constantine,* 296 U.S. 287, 294; *Carter* v. *Carter Coal Co.,* 298 U.S. 238, 289.

the law ought to be; he must have recourse to the principles of morality." [38] No doubt a judge must dispose of any controversy that he has been given jurisdiction to decide and must base his judgment on law of some sort. However, I cannot suppose that he must snatch a meaning from any gibberish that may emanate from a legislature. In our system at any rate a party asking relief must be able to satisfy the court that there is a command that he shall have it, and he loses if he fails to do so as much as though he failed in proving his facts. Moreover, it is seldom that a statute is so obscure that a court finds it inscrutable, and in any event that is not the situation I have in mind. It is of course true that when a court holds that a legislature has left too much latitude to an administrative tribunal, it overrules a decision of the legislature as to its powers; but there appears to me a tenable distinction between that situation and one where a court overrules the actual exercise of legislative authority; for the delegation of authority is *pro tanto* the abdication of authority over the subject matter by a transfer to others of authority that the legislature alone may exercise. Once we assume that courts are to set the boundaries of each "Department's" authority, it follows that they must say where legislation begins, however hazy its boundaries may be.

[38] *Nature and Sources of Law,* §642.

There have been much more than intimations of a stiffer interpretation of the "Due Process Clause," when the subject matter is not Property but Liberty, as that word has now come to be defined. It would indeed be too much to say that the Supreme Court has definitively and irrevocably committed itself to a difference, but certainly at the moment that seems likely. In part this has probably arisen from the specific prohibitions in the First Amendment against the "free exercise of religion" or any "abridgement of the freedom of speech or of the press." But the Court's language is general and, if taken as authoritative, asserts a much wider authority to reverse the legislative choice between conflicting values when these are "personal." Moreover, it has now become apparently accepted doctrine that the "Due Process Clause" in the Fourteenth Amendment covers the prohibitions of the First.[39] Indeed, if one were to take literally some of the language, there would be reason to say that the Fourteenth Amendment now had in its bosom all the first eight.

I cannot help thinking that it would have seemed a strange anomaly to those who penned the words in the Fifth to learn that they constituted severer restrictions as to Liberty than Property, especially now

---

[39] *Near* v. *Minnesota,* 283 U.S. 697, 707; *De Jonge* v. *Oregon,* 299 U.S. 353, 364; *Schneider* v. *State,* 308 U.S. 147, 160; *Thornhill* v. *Alabama,* 310 U.S. 88, 95.

that Liberty not only includes freedom from personal restraint, but enough economic security to allow its possessor the enjoyment of a satisfactory life. I can see no more persuasive reason for supposing that a legislature is *a priori* less qualified to choose between "personal" than between economic values; and there have been strong protests, to me unanswerable, that there is no constitutional basis for asserting a larger measure of judicial supervision over the first than over the second. Consider, for example, the contrasting opinions in *Board of Education* v. *Barnette*,[40] in which the majority avowedly overruled a recent decision of the Court. The majority spoke thus (p. 648):

"The test of legislation which collides with the Fourteenth Amendment because it also collides with the principles of the First, is much more definite than the test when only the Fourteenth is involved. Much of the vagueness of the due process clause disappears when the specific prohibitions of the First become its standard. The right of a State to regulate, for example, a public utility may well include, so far as the due process test is concerned, power to impose all of the restrictions which a legislature may have a 'rational basis' for adopting. But freedoms of speech and of press, of assembly, and of worship may not be infringed on such slender

[40] 319 U.S. 624.

51

grounds. They are susceptible of restriction only to prevent grave and immediate danger."

Contrast that language with that of one of the dissenters (p. 648):

"There is no warrant in the constitutional basis of this Court's authority for attributing different roles to it, depending upon the nature of the challenge to the legislation. Our power does not vary according to the particular provision of the Bill of Rights which is invoked. The right not to have property taken without just compensation has, so far as the right to be compensated is concerned, the same constitutional dignity as the right to be protected against unreasonable searches and seizures, and the latter has no less claim than freedom of the press or freedom of speech, or religious freedom."

Finally, although the language of the majority appears to have been accepted in at least three later decisions,[41] when in 1950 the prevailing opinion in *Ullmann* v. *United States* [42] declared that "as no constitutional guarantee enjoys preference, so none should suffer subordination or deletion," only one of the seven who made up the majority singled that statement out for dissent. It must be confessed that

[41] *Murdock* v. *Pennsylvania*, 319 U.S. 105, 115; *Thomas* v. *Collins*, 323 U.S. 516, 530; *Kovacs* v. *Cooper*, 336 U.S. 77, 88.
[42] 350 U.S. 422, 428.

at least twenty years ago the notion had been forward that the Fourteenth Amendment, aside from whether it incorporated the First, gi much wider scope for judicial intervention v the choices are between "personal" values. How are we to read, for example, the following langi from a justice by no means given to the extr assertion of judicial intervention? [43]

"We reach a different plane of social and m values when we pass to the privileges and imm ties that have taken over from the earlier article the federal bill of rights and brought within Fourteenth Amendment by a process of absorpt ... the process of absorption has had its sourc the belief that neither liberty nor justice wo exist if they were sacrificed. . . . So it has come ab that the domain of liberty withdrawn by the Fo teenth Amendment from encroachments by states has been enlarged by latter-day judgment include liberty of the mind as well as libert action. The extension indeed, became a logical perative when once it was recognized, as long a was, that liberty is something more than exem from physical restraint, and even in the field o stantive rights and duties the legislative judg if oppressive and arbitrary, may be overridd the courts."

[43] *Palko* v. *Connecticut*, 302 U.S. 319, 326, 327.

racial equality is a paramount value that state legislatures are not to appraise and whose invasion is fatal to the validity of any statute. Whether the result would have been the same if the interests involved had been economic, of course I cannot say, but there can be no doubt that at least as to "Personal Rights" the old doctrine seems to have been reasserted. It is curious that no mention was made of section five, which offered an escape from intervening, for it empowers Congress to "enforce" all the preceding sections by "appropriate legislation." The Court must have regarded this as only a cumulative corrective, not being disposed to divest itself of that power of review that it has so often exercised and as often disclaimed.

I must therefore conclude this part of what I have to say by acknowledging that I do not know what the doctrine is as to the scope of these clauses; I cannot frame any definition that will explain when the Court will assume the role of a third legislative chamber and when it will limit its authority to keeping Congress and the states within their accredited authority. Nevertheless, I am quite clear that it has not abdicated its former function, as to which I hope that it may be regarded as permissible for me to say that I have never been able to understand on what basis it does or can rest except as a *coup de main*.

III

The Guardians

In my first lecture I tried to state the justification under our system for the courts' power to annul a federal or state statute because it is contrary to the Constitution. In my second lecture I discussed what are the conditions upon which this power should be exercised when it is based upon the "Due Process Clause" or the "Equal Protection Clause," between which I do not distinguish. In this lecture I shall say first why I do not think that the interests mentioned in the First Amendment are entitled in point of constitutional interpretation to a measure of protection different from other interests; and then conclude by considering whether, even assuming that I am right in thinking that the Constitution does not warrant the courts in annulling any legislation because they disapprove it on the merits, nevertheless it is desirable that they should exercise such an authority on extreme occasions.

At first blush it seems plausible to distinguish between the "Due Process Clause" and the two provisions of the First Amendment forbidding Congress to pass any law (1) "prohibiting the free exercise of religion," and (2) "abridging the freedom of speech or of the press." These are specific interests and the prohibition is in form unconditional. First as to Speech. That privilege rests upon the premise that there is no proposition so uniformly acknowledged that it may not be lawfully challenged, questioned, and debated. It need not rest upon the further premise that there are no propositions that are not open to doubt; it is enough, even if there are, that in the end it is worse to suppress dissent than to run the risk of heresy. Hence it has been again and again unconditionally proclaimed that there are no limits to the privilege so far as words seek to affect only the hearers' beliefs and not their conduct. The trouble is that conduct is almost always based upon some belief, and that to change the hearer's belief will generally to some extent change his conduct, and may even evoke conduct that the law forbids. Everyone agrees that there may be so close a causal sequence between the belief engendered and the unlawful conduct as to toll the privilege; but what that sequence must be still remains obscure.

Let me approach by steps. Suppose the words are such that, if the hearer acted upon the belief they induced, the speaker would become a principal in a crime. There are such words, as everyone agrees; indeed, the existing federal statute defines them in terms that in substance go back at least to the time of Bracton.[46] One makes himself a principal in the commission of a crime by the hearer when he "aids, abets, counsels, commands or procures" the hearer to commit it.[47] As you will observe, several, if not all, of these acts may be only verbal. I am not aware that anyone has ever suggested that, although the utterance induces the hearer to attempt to commit the crime, it is privileged if the attempt fails. Nor have I ever heard that even the most ardent champions of the privilege extend it to words that, though they fail to persuade the hearer to attempt to commit the crime, would make him a principal if they had succeeded in inducing him to make an attempt.

So far we seem to be on terra firma. On the other hand there have been, and still are, those who believe that words will be privileged, even though they satisfy the definition, if the unlawful conduct they seek to induce is to be after a substantial interval. That is the doctrine of "clear and present danger." The only ground for this exception that I have ever heard is that during the interval between the provocation and its realization correctives may

46 *United States* v. *Peoni,* 100 Fed. 2d 401 (C.C.A. 2).
47 Section 2 (a), Title 18, U.S.C.

arise, and that it is better to accept the risk that they may not be sufficient than to suppress what, however guilty in itself, may prove innocuous. I confess that I cannot understand why it should not be adequate protection of the speaker's privilege if he were allowed to show that the interval made it reasonably certain that the provocation would not be realized. It is always a difficult matter to forecast what will be the effect of such a pause, and by hypothesis the words proceed from an unlawful purpose and do not therefore fall within any interest that the amendment is designed to protect. I doubt that the doctrine will persist, and I cannot help thinking that for once Homer nodded.

In *Yates* v. *United States*,[48] the Supreme Court made a distinction between words that advocate "concrete action" and those that advocate "principles divorced from action." It would be difficult, indeed perhaps it would be impossible, to imagine an occasion on which the statute would make the advocate of "principles divorced from action" a principal in a crime, even though his words had in fact provoked the hearer to commit it; but there are occasions, I submit, when the speaker may lose his privilege although he confines himself to "principles divorced from action." Let me suggest a not impos-

[48] 354 U.S. 298.

59

sible one on which such an utterance would not I believe be protected. Suppose that a man wished to denounce the ineptitude and corruption of the government to a crowd that he knew to be ripe for riot; and that he had been told that what he proposed to say would probably set them off. Suppose farther that he still persisted in going on with his speech because he believed he had a message of high importance. Would it be privileged? It merely states the problem to say that the answer turns on "whether the gravity of the 'evil' discounted by its improbability justifies such invasion of free speech as is necessary to avoid the danger." [49] I cannot improve upon Professor Freund's gloss:

"The truth is that the clear-and-present danger test is an over-simplified judgment unless it takes account also of a number of other factors: the relative seriousness of the danger in comparison with the value of the occasion for speech or political activity; the availability of more moderate controls than those which the state has imposed; and perhaps the specific intent with which the speech or activity is launched. No matter how rapidly we utter the phrase 'clear and present danger,' or how closely we hyphenate the words, they are not a substitute for the weighing of values. They tend to convey a delusion of certainty when what is most certain is the complexity of the

[49] *Dennis* v. *United States,* 341 U.S. 494, 510.

aries other than that there shall have been an honest effort to weigh the values according to the prevalent mores. *Butler* v. *Michigan* [52] does not deal with the question; the Supreme Court held a Michigan statute invalid under the "Due Process Clause" because it restrained the circulation among adults of books not objectionable as to them, but forbidden in order to prevent their reaching children. It may indeed well be asked why, if the end was lawful, as the Court assumed, there should be a judicial review of the means adopted by the legislature. The state court may have been wrong in its interpretation of the statute, but as so interpreted did it offend the "Due Process Clause," however inappropriate the means?

The last word upon the question is *Roth* v. *United States,* [53] in which the Court upheld (1) a federal statute that used as definition, "obscene, lewd, lascivious or filthy," [54] and (2) a state statute that merely used the words, "obscene or indecent." [55] In the first case the judge had left to the jury to say whether the words were such as to "offend the common conscience of the community by present-day standards" of which the jury were "the exclusive judges"; in the second the charge was whether it had

[52] 352 U.S. 380.   [53] 354 U.S. 476.
[54] Section 1461, Title 18 U.S.C.
[55] West's California Penal Code, §311.

strands in the web of freedom that the ju
disentangle."[50]

The controversy may arise over a statut
cally covering the occasion, and the quest
then be the same as on occasions when th
Process Clause is involved. The standard set
prevail unless the court is satisfied that it w
the product of an effort impartially to balan
conflicting values. When the statute does n
down a standard specifically covering the occa
the court must of course first "interpret" it,
should it conclude that it does cover the occasio
cannot see why it should dispose of the dispute
any different test.

So much for words that provoke their hearers
unlawful conduct. What of those that may b
thought to have an evil effect upon their morals
generally because they arouse lascivious emotions?
The publication of these was a crime at common
law, and the Supreme Court has very recently held
that when a "legislative body concludes that the
mores of the community call for an extension of the
impermissible limits, an enactment aimed at the
evil is plainly within its power, if it does not trans-
gress the boundaries fixed by the Constitution for
freedom of expression." [51] I know of no such bound-

50 Freund, *On Understanding the Supreme Court,* pp. 27, 28.
51 *Winters* v. *New York,* 333 U.S. 507, 515.

"a substantial tendency to deprave or corrupt the readers by inciting lascivious thoughts or by arousing lustful desires."

The objections had been two: (1) that the statutes, so construed, covered material that might not have any effect upon the readers' conduct; and (2) that the test was too uncertain. The Court disposed of the second objection by adverting to the well-settled doctrine that statutes often impose on the individual the risk of ascertaining what are the current mores, and allow only as mitigating circumstances his personal failure to comprehend them. To the first objection it replied that it had been the long established habit of most societies to suppress language likely to arouse lewd emotions; and that this might be a lawfully protected interest regardless of any conduct that would result. So far as appears from these decisions, it is for the legislature to determine what are the not "impermissible limits" by balancing the evil of those lustful emotions that the language may excite against depriving the author and his audience of the benefit of what he has to say.

Essentially the same considerations apply to laws "respecting an establishment of religion or prohibiting the free exercise thereof," for here too there are no absolutes, and it is a question of balancing conflicting values. We have forbidden polygamy, though it was an honestly entertained article of the Mormon creed. Obviously we should forbid suttee, hara kiri, or such self-mutilation as in the past was a common practice in the worship of Adonis. We could, though we do not, lawfully require all citizens to do military service regardless of their religious principles, and we put conscientious objectors in prison if they refuse to perform duties that are auxiliary to success in our prosecution of a war. We compel people to be vaccinated and to provide medical attention to their children, although it may be against their religious convictions to do so.

It is perhaps still doubtful how far we may go to control the manner in which religious teaching may be spread,[56] but there can be no doubt that there are limits. For example, if airplanes hovered over cities through the night bellowing forth religious propaganda, I cannot doubt that it would be constitutional to stop them. Again I should hesitate to say, at least, if no "prior restraint" were involved, and if some more definite word than "sacrilegious" were used to describe the offense,[57] that a statute would be invalid that forbade the broadcasting of vituperation of a rival religion, no matter how disgusting the vilification might be.[58] Certainly the line between this and such outbursts as are likely

[56] *Saia* v. *New York,* 334 U.S. 558; *Kovacs* v. *Cooper,* 336 U.S. 77.
[57] *Joseph Burstyn, Inc.* v. *Wilson,* 343 U.S. 495.
[58] *Kunz* v. *New York,* 340 U.S. 290.

to provoke disorder has proved difficult to draw.[59]

Finally, consider the equivocation with which the prohibition of the "establishment of any religion" is enforced. It is generally, if not universally, conceded that church property, at least the land on which the edifice stands, is tax exempt, which is a subsidy in all but name; yet there seems to be a wide division of opinion as to whether free buses to religious schools are forbidden. Similarly, as to whether public school buildings may be used for religious instructions and whether it is permissible to count as the equivalent of the time that children must attend school, time spent in religious instruction outside school.[60]

The other provisions of the first eight amendments except perhaps the last are all addressed to specific occasions and have no such scope as those I have mentioned. Many of them embody political victories of the seventeenth century over the Crown, and carry their own nimbus of precedent. So far as they do, any extension beyond their historical meaning seems to me unwarranted, though that limitation is not always observed. It is true that at times they may present issues not unlike those that arise under the First Amendment and the "Due

[59] *Feiner* v. *New York,* 340 U.S. 315.

[60] *Everson* v. *Board of Education,* 330 U.S. 1; *Illinois ex rel. McCollum* v. *Board of Education,* 333 U.S. 203; *Zorach* v. *Clauson,* 343 U.S. 306.

Process Clause," and in such cases I cannot see why courts should intervene, unless it appears that the statutes are not honest choices between values and sacrifices honestly appraised.

May I crave your patience while I recapitulate what I have so far tried to say? The authority of courts to annul statutes (and *a fortiori,* acts of the Executive) may, and indeed must, be inferred, although it is nowhere expressed, for without it we should have to refer all disputes between the "Departments" and states to popular decision, patently an impractical means of relief, whatever Thomas Jefferson may have thought. However, this power should be confined to occasions when the statute or order was outside the grant of power to the grantee, and should not include a review of how the power has been exercised. This distinction in the case of legislation demands an analysis of its component factors. These are an estimate of the relevant existing facts and a forecast of the changes that the proposed measure will bring about. In addition it involves an appraisal of the values that the change will produce, as to which there are no postulates specific enough to serve as guides on concrete occasions. In the end all that can be asked on review by a court is that the appraisals and the choice shall be impartial. The statute may be far from the best solution of the conflicts with which it deals; but if it is the result of an honest effort to embody that compromise or adjustment that will secure the widest acceptance and most avoid resentment, it is "Due Process of Law" and conforms to the First Amendment. In theory any statute is always open to challenge upon the ground that it was not in truth the result of an impartial effort, but from the outset it was seen that any such inquiry was almost always practically impossible, and moreover it would be to the last degree "political."

I am well aware that the decisions do not so narrowly circumscribe the power of courts to intervene under the authority of the First Amendment and the "Due Process Clause." I have not tried to say how far those decisions have in fact extended the scope of these clauses. Frankly, I should despair of succeeding. On the contrary I have been only trying to say what is the measure of judicial intervention that can be thought to be implicit, though unexpressed, in the Constitution. You may well ask, however, what difference it makes at long last if the courts do exceed those implicit limits. Even though until about a century ago it was the accepted role of courts to confine themselves to occasions when Congress or the states had stepped over their borders, why should we now retreat, if it has become the custom to go further and correct patent deviations from a court's notions of justice? It is a "constitution," you may go on to remind me, that we are "expounding," and constitutions have the habit of organic growth. Ours is no different from other constitutions, and it has by now been modified to protect the basic privileges of any free society by means of an agency made irresponsive to the pressure of public hysteria, public panic and public greed.

There may be much to be said for the existence of some such organ in a democratic state, especially if its power be confined to a suspensive veto, like that for example of the present British House of Lords. The recuperative powers of a government that has no such curb are indeed great, but in the interval between the damage and the restoration great permanent injury may be done, and in any event the suffering of individuals will never be repaired. Those who advocate such relief at times concede too scanty importance to the provisions very carefully devised at least in the federal Constitution to check hasty and ill-considered legislation. The veto and independent tenure of the President, unlike that of the ministry in most democracies, are obvious curbs upon sudden swings of popular obsession; so too is the Senate, whose control is in the hands of a small minority of the population, representing a facet of public opinion quite different from that of the urban sections. However, I am not going to discuss whether it might not be desirable to have a third chamber, but on the contrary I shall assume for argument that it would be. The question still remains whether the courts should be that chamber. Let me try to sum up the case on both sides: and first that of those who wish to give the courts power to review the merits.

I agree that they have the better argument so far as concerns Free Speech. The most important issues here arise when a majority of the voters are hostile, often bitterly hostile, to the dissidents against whom the statute is directed; and legislatures are more likely than courts to repress what ought to be free. It is true that the periods of passion or panic are ordinarily not very long, and that they are usually succeeded by a serener and more tolerant temper; but, as I have just said, serious damage may have been done that cannot be undone, and no restitution is ordinarily possible for the individuals who have suffered. This is a substantial and important advantage of wide judicial review.

When one comes to the other interests covered by the "Bill of Rights" it seems to me impossible to be sure on which side the advantage lies. Judges are perhaps more apt than legislators to take a long view, but that varies so much with the individual that generalization is hazardous. We are faced with the ever present problem in all popular government: how far the will of immediate majorities should prevail. Even assuming, as I am, that a suspensive veto would be desirable, the power to annul a statute is much more than that. It does not send back the challenged measure for renewed deliberation; it forbids it by making a different appraisal of the values, which, as I have just said, is the essence of legislation. Moreover, judges are seldom content merely to annul the particular solution before them; they do not, indeed they may not, say that taking all things into consideration, the legislators' solution is too strong for the judicial stomach. On the contrary they wrap up their veto in a protective veil of adjectives such as "arbitrary," "artificial," "normal," "reasonable," "inherent," "fundamental," or "essential," whose office usually, though quite innocently, is to disguise what they are doing and impute to it a derivation far more impressive than their personal preferences, which are all that in fact lie behind the decision. If we do need a third chamber it should appear for what it is, and not as the interpreter of inscrutable principles.

Another supposed advantage of the wider power of review seems to be that by "the moral radiation of its decision" a court may point the way to a resolution of the social conflicts involved better than any likely to emerge from a legislature. In other words, courts may light the way to a saner world and ought to be encouraged to do so. I should indeed be glad to believe it, and it may be that my failure hitherto to observe it is owing to some personal defect of vision; but at any rate judges have large areas left unoccupied by legislation within which to exercise this benign function. Besides, for a judge to serve as communal mentor appears to me a very dubious addition to his duties and one apt to interfere with their proper discharge.

So much for the advantages that may result from a judicial review. In what respect is it inexpedient? In the first place it is apparent, I submit, that in so far as it is made part of the duties of judges to take sides in political controversies, their known or expected convictions or predilections will, and indeed should, be at least one determinant in their appointment and an important one. There has been plenty of past experience that confirms this; indeed, we have become so used to it that we accept it as a matter of course. No doubt it is inevitable, however circumscribed his duty may be, that the personal proclivities of an interpreter will to some extent interject themselves into the meaning he imputes to a text, but in very much the greater part of a judge's duties he is charged with freeing himself as far as he can from all personal preferences, and that becomes difficult in proportion as these are strong. The degree to which he will secure compliance with his commands depends in large measure upon how far the com-

munity believes him to be the mouthpiece of a
public will, conceived as the resultant of many conflicting strains that have come, at least provisionally,
to a consensus. This sanction disappears in so far as
it is supposed permissible for him covertly to smuggle
into his decisions his personal notions of what is desirable, however disinterested personally those may
be. Compliance will then much more depend upon a
resort to force, not a desirable expedient when it
can be avoided.

This consideration becomes especially important
in appellate courts. It is often hard to secure unanimity about the borders of legislative power, but that is
much easier than to decide how far a particular adjustment diverges from what the judges deem toler-
able. On such issues experience has over and over
again shown the difficulty of securing unanimity.
This is disastrous because disunity cancels the impact of monolithic solidarity on which the authority
of a bench of judges so largely depends. People become aware that the answer to the controversy is
uncertain, even to those best qualified, and they feel
free, unless especially docile, to ignore it if they are
reasonably sure that they will not be caught. The
reasoning of both sides is usually beyond their com-
prehension, and is apt to appear as verbiage designed to sustain one side of a dispute that in the end
might be decided either way, which is generally the

truth. Moreover, it certainly does not accord with the underlying presuppositions of popular government to vest in a chamber, unaccountable to anyone but itself, the power to suppress social experiments which it does not approve. Nothing, I submit, could warrant such a censorship except a code of paramount law that not only measured the scope of legislative authority but regulated how it should be exercised.

Each one of us must in the end choose for himself how far he would like to leave our collective fate to the wayward vagaries of popular assemblies. No one can fail to recognize the perils to which the last forty years have exposed such governments. We are not indeed forced to choose between absolutism and the kind of democracy that so often prevailed in Greek cities during the sixth to fourth centuries before our era. The Founding Fathers were acutely, perhaps overacutely, aware of the dangers that had followed that sort of rule, though, as you all know, they differed widely as to what curbs to impose. For myself it would be most irksome to be ruled by a bevy of Platonic Guardians, even if I knew how to choose them, which I assuredly do not. If they were in charge, I should miss the stimulus of living in a society where I have, at least theoretically, some part in the direction of public affairs. Of course I know how illusory would be the belief that my vote determined anything; but nevertheless when I go to the polls I have a satisfaction in the sense that we are all engaged in a common venture. If you retort that a sheep in the flock may feel something like it; I reply, following Saint Francis, "My brother, the Sheep."

I have tried to strike a balance between the advantages of our own system and one in which we might enjoy at least the protection of judges against our frailties. To me it seems better to take our chances that such constitutional restraints as already exist may not sufficiently arrest the recklessness of popular assemblies. If we can find time for some other activity than forging fantastic engines of war and using them to destroy each other, who knows but we shall acquire so intimate an acquaintance with ourselves that we shall indeed discover principles that will be as objectively valid as those that govern inanimate things; and if so, perhaps Mr. Aldous Huxley's mescaline, or Mr. Gordon Wasson's mushrooms will then help to get them generally accepted. Meanwhile, I can think of nothing better than to stake our future upon conclusions about ourselves that we must recognize as provisional, as no better than surmises which we must never weary of putting to a test. Listen to the words of the wisest of the Founding Fathers — Benjamin Franklin. The Convention had finally agreed upon the form of the Constitution. It was engrossed and the vote was to be taken on Monday, September 17th, 1787. Franklin had written out his reasons for voting in the affirmative. Wilson read them to the Convention because the old man did not feel quite able to make the effort. They completely represent the combination of tolerance and imagination that to me is the epitome of all good government, when coupled with the rare courage that, as Holmes used to put it, will risk life on a conclusion that tomorrow may disprove. I ask you to bear with me while I read the greater part of it, for it will not bear much condensing.

"Mr. President, I confess that there are several parts of this constitution which I do not at present approve, but I am not sure that I shall never approve them: For, having lived long, I have experienced many instances of being obliged by better information or fuller consideration to change opinions even on important subjects, which I once thought right, but found to be otherwise. It is therefore that the older I grow, the more apt I am to doubt my own judgment, and to pay more respect to the judgment of others. Most men indeed as well as most sects in Religion, think themselves in the possession of all truth and that whatever others differ from them it is so far error.... In these sentiments, Sir, I agree to this Constitution with all its faults, if they are such, because I think a general Government necessary for us and there is no form of Government but what may be a blessing to the people if well administered, and believe farther that this is likely to be well administered for a course of years, and can only end in Despotism, as other forms have done before it, when the people have become so corrupted as to need despotic Government, being incapable of any other. I doubt too whether any other Convention we can obtain may be able to make a better Constitution. For when you assemble a number of men to have the advantage of their joint wisdom, you inevitably assemble with those men, all their prejudices, their passions, their errors of opinion, their local interests, and their selfishness. From such an Assembly can a perfect production be expected? It therefore astonishes me, Sir, to find this system approaching so near to perfection as it does and I think it will astonish our enemies, who are waiting with confidence to hear that our councils are confounded like those of the Builders of Babel; and that our States are on the point of separation, only to meet hereafter for the purpose of cutting one another's throats. Thus I consent, Sir, to this Constitution because I expect no better, and because I am not sure it is not the best. . . . On the whole, Sir, I cannot help expressing a wish that every member of the Convention who may still have objections to it, would with me, on this occasion doubt a little of his own infallibility — and to make manifest our unanimity, put his name to this instrument."

More years ago than I like now to remember I sat in this building and listened to — yes, more than that, was dissected by — men all but one of whom are now dead. What I got from them was not alone the Rule in Shelley's case, or what was one's duty to an invited person — as we then called him — or what law determined whether a contract has been made, or how inadequate was the common law of partnership before the advent of Cory on Accounts, or in what jurisdictions a corporation is "present." True, I did get those so far as I was able to absorb them, but I got much more. I carried away the impress of a band of devoted scholars; patient, considerate, courteous and kindly, whom nothing could daunt and nothing could bribe. The memory of those men has been with me ever since. Again and again they have helped me when the labor seemed heavy, the task seemed trivial, and the confusion seemed indecipherable. From them I learned that it is as craftsmen that we get our satisfactions and our pay. In the universe of truth they lived by the sword; they asked no quarter of absolutes and they gave none. Go ye and do likewise.

Table of Cases

78

TABLE OF CASES

LEARNED HAND, born in Albany, New York, in 1872, and a graduate of the college and of the law school of Harvard University, was U. S. District Judge for fifteen years and Judge of the U. S. Circuit Court for the 2nd Circuit for twenty-seven years before his retirement in 1951. During his long service and in the years of his retirement, he was one of the most respected and influential jurists in the English-speaking world.

CHARLES EDWARD WYZANSKI, JR. was born in Boston in 1906, received his collegiate and legal education at Harvard. His posts in government included those of Solicitor in the Department of Labor, and Special Assistant to the U. S. Attorney General. Since 1941, he has been U. S. District Judge for Massachusetts. Judge Wyzanski is a member of the Council of the American Law Institute.